Infinity Across Infinity

Syed Ahmad Muzzammil

BookLeaf
Publishing

India | USA | UK

Made with ❤ on the BookLeaf Publishing Platform
www.bookleafpub.in
www.bookleafpub.com

Dedication

To the ones we love, the ones we lost, and the ones who remain unnamed in our hearts. To fleeting moments, unspoken words, and memories that refuse to fade with the the passing of. This is for every soul that has loved someone or something beyond time, across infinity.

Preface

Poetry is a voyage—one that transcends time, space, and emotion. *Infinity Across Infinity* is not just a collection of poems but a journey through love, longing, self-discovery, and rebellion. Each verse is a fragment of my soul, a reflection of moments lived, lost, and dreamt.

This book is an exploration of the infinite—the vastness of emotions that stretch beyond words, the echoes of memories that refuse to fade, and the spaces between us that hold unspoken truths. Some poems may whisper of heartbreak, others of hope; some may rebel, while others surrender to destiny. But all of them, in some way, are pieces of an infinite love story, a longing that knows no bounds.

I invite you to walk through these pages, to find your own meanings within the verses, and to lose yourself in the rhythm of infinity. For poetry, like love, exists beyond time—reaching across infinity to those willing to listen.

—Syed Ahmad Muzzammil

Acknowledgements

No journey is ever taken alone, and this book is no
exception.
To the ones who inspired these words—you may or may
not know it, but you live in these pages, in the spaces
between the lines, in the silences that speak as loudly as
the verses themselves.

To my family, my friends and well-wishers, who have
read my work, shared their thoughts, and stood by me
through this creative endeavor—thank you for being my
sounding board, my critics, and my biggest cheerleaders.

A special thanks to those who walked into my life,
leaving behind moments worth immortalizing in poetry.
Whether through love or loss, your presence has shaped
these verses in ways words cannot fully express.

And finally, to you—the reader. Thank you for holding
this book in your hands, for giving my words a home in
your heart. This book is as much yours as it is mine.

With gratitude,
Syed Ahmad Muzzammil

1. I Want You, Forever

As the sunlight in early morning, I crave you,
And like the moon that softens the night, I long for you.
The way the earth clings to its axis, I hold on to you.
I want you in the stillness of midnight,
Before my day begins, and when it fades into dusk,
I want you.
When joy fills my heart, I want you.
And when the weight of the world bears down, I need
you.
My shrink, my friend, my confidante—
I need you.
I want you in ways that give
a dying soul a reason to breathe,
and a fleeing soldier, a cause worth fighting for.
I want you—
selfishly, exclusively.
I want you by my side, your fingers laced with mine.
At the door as I leave, and beside me in the car I drive.
On the path I walk, and at the place I finally rest.
I want you to whisper *goodnight* like a quiet prayer.
I want my mornings bathed in gratitude—
thanking the universe for one more day with you.
My evenings, sipping coffee from your hands,
your head a gentle weight on my shoulder.

I want you—
unconditionally, irrevocably.
I want to listen to your dreams, and all your fears.
I want you to know—your secrets are safe with me.
And sometimes, I want nothing at all,
just to lose myself in your face,
for hours and hours—
as if staring long enough
might etch you into my eternity.
I want to grow old with you,
to collect memories like fallen leaves,
as many as the lines time carves upon our skin.
I want you a thousand times.
I want you endlessly,
with every breath, every heartbeat, every second.
Right or wrong—I do not care.
All I know is this—
I want you.
My existence, my soul, every fiber of me
feels undone without you.
Beyond all the words I know,
beyond all I can express or comprehend,
I want you.
Today, tomorrow, forever—
I want you.

2. Everything Is You

The poems I write
are nothing
but beautiful memories of you.
The stories they tell
are my way of keeping you alive in my heart.
The metaphors I weave in words
are the imprints you left on my soul.
And the pain that lingers in every line
is my craving—my endless longing for you.
My everything is you...!!

3. Stars Could Speak

If only
these stars knew how to speak,
they would tell you stories
Far away, somewhere,
there lives a man
who falls asleep loving you,
lost in your thoughts,
drifting between the beautiful hope
of seeing you someday
and the excruciating pain of your absence today.
If only stars could tell stories,
they would whisper tales
of selfless, passionate,
unflinching, irrevocable love
a love they witness every night.
But you remain unaware
of all that belongs to you,
and to you alone.

4. One Day, My Love

One day, my love,
At the stroke of midnight,
Under the moonlight
And a clear night sky,
With stars twinkling bright,
You may step onto your balcony,
Gazing at the beauty of the majestic night,
Unaware that behind the lamppost before you,
A man stands, holding his breath,
Having travelled a thousand miles
And crossed seven seas,
Just to catch a glimpse
Of your moonlit face
And twinkling eyes.

5. Dance With Me

Dance with me,
to eternity.
On a floor scattered with stardust,
under magical lamps
yellow, red, and purple.
Your favorite music playing on a guitar,
my favorite dance partner, you are.
I am holding my breath...
Would you hold my hand
and dance?
Dance with me,
to eternity.

6. Dar Bistro & Books

This beautiful café, on a November evening,
Wooden walls bathed in yellow moonlight.
I sit at a corner table,
Lost in the crowd that doesn't notice me,
Yet noticing every face, listening to every voice.
Eyes seeking, heart racing,
Mind wondering..!!
"Will she come?"
In a WhatsApp chat, on a gloomy day,
Maybe a year and a half ago,
She had said, perhaps casually,
"We'll go to this café one day."
Still warm are those vivid memories of you,
Unlike this coffee, forgotten and cold.
Midnight now—faces fade, voices dim,
One by one, they all leave.
I will come again, on another evening,
For the same song, the same dance,
A false hope, a wishful thought.

7. That Sea Beach Near Your Office

A mundane day at the office,
Where you're a captive of the same **workflows**, **activities**,
and **sequences**.
Anaconda and **Python** strangling you,
Peculiar bugs biting through the **error logs**,
And coffee breaks no longer working their magic.
When life's meaning gets lost beneath thousands of **ifs**
and **elses**,
When every **foreach** goal you set feels distant,
Looping endlessly in an infinite cycle,
Take a **break statement** from work,
And **GoTo** that sea beach you once told me about.
Walk, walk barefoot.
Let the waves kiss your feet.
Be still for a moment—take a long, deep breath.
Let the wind play with your skirt and hair.
Stretch your arms wide and feel, feel me.
From a thousand miles away,
I send this water and breeze to caress you.
The vast, unending sea, this is how much I love you...!!
And like its depth, swallowing mighty ships and vessels,
I will take in all your agony, stress, and worries.
Like the sand slipping beneath your feet,

Let all your burdens drift into the sea.

Now, like a mermaid

Beautiful and free,

Mystical and magnificent,

Magical and enchanting,

Go chase your dreams like they're brand new.

8. You Are...!!

You are not just memories,
Not merely a person or a companion.
You are not a feeling—
Something that comes and goes.
Not a habit, desire, or dream either,
As they change.
You are fused into my soul—inseparable.
You are what makes me whole when you're with me,
And what makes me incomplete when you're not

9. Undefined

Undefined is your absence
the hollow I feel, even in a crowd, full of people
at a party alive with laughter,
yet I am wrapped in loneliness.
Undefined is the comfort
of being in your arms,
the touch of your hands,
the night you first held mine.
Undefined are the joys
of walking with you by my side
through dark lanes, endless highways,
reaching your doorstep yet hesitating to leave,
lingering, stalling, saying, *"Let's Walk just a little more."*
Undefined is your place in my life,
your existence tied to my survival,
your presence the air I breathe.
Undefined is what you are to me,
the bond we share,
no word ever spoken, or language ever known,
could capture what I feel for you.
And even if I tried,
it would always be an understatement.

10. Bon Voyage My Love

Untamed, rebellious, surrendering to none,
Such are the traits you were given.
Never have you allowed yourself to be driven
By society's trivial conventions.
You've left behind your native land,
Chasing the horizon, bound for a rough voyage.
I see you've made two companions—
The wind and the water.
The wind flirts with you, playing with your skirt and
hair,
While the water holds your ship firm.
But when they reveal their true forms—
When the wind turns to violent turbulence,
And the water rises to the sky,
Dragging you toward its unfathomable depths—
Do not be afraid, for you are not alone.
A guardian angel I may not be,
But a rogue from demons' clan.
With God's grace and all my strength,
I shall hold the ship's sail up and steady—
Against the current, against the wind,
We shall press forward together.
And when the waters fall silent, cold as death,
I shall hold you close,

Whispering the songs you love—
"No Need to Say Goodbye", "Underneath Your Clothes."
And when thirst haunts you with no relief,
I shall barter my blood with the creatures of the deep,
Dive down where hidden streams of fresh water flow.
And when night falls, dark as blindness,
I shall set my wings on fire—
To light your path and guide your journey.
But when the storm calms,
When the wind carries you gently forward,
When the sea becomes as serene as your divine face,
Knowing you no longer need me,
I shall vanish, silently, into thin air.
Yet, if your heart desires not just the land of your dreams,
But an endless voyage with me by your side,
You need only say—
"I love you. Don't go away."
But before I leave, before I go,
Let me embrace you once and say just two words—
"BON VOYAGE," my love.

11. Without You

In the mountains and by the city's sea shore,
On a jungle trek or in a bookstore,
The journey, the search, the companion—it's all you.
So don't ask me how I do without you.
My flesh and bones, aspirations and desires,
The promises I make, the secrets I keep,
Everywhere I go and everything I do,
In one way or another, they all lead to you.
So don't ask me how I do without you.
It matters least, so remain unaware
Of all that you mean and all you could be.
For my love, my emotions, my care
Aren't bound by the trivialities of time and distance—
Not even by acknowledgment from you.
Unnoticed, unspoken, untold,
But always and forever, it shall be with you.
From halfway across the world, infinity times infinity, I
will miss you.
Till my last dying breath, I will hold dear and vivid, all
my memories of you.
And perhaps, on my unmarked grave, they would place a
stone inscribed—
"Do not ask me how I do without you."

12. Metamorphosis

The high waves of my imagination,
The giant tides of my longings,
Find their peace as they descend
Upon the golden blaze of your coast.
My ever-wandering soul,
My never-ending quest,
Harbors itself, anchors its station,
In the city you call your abode.
Desire for an inamorata,
Craving for a paramour,
Finds solace only when
The warmth of your soul
Briskly blends into mine.
Yet at times, you seem a stranger,
Someone I can barely recognize.
You may try to conceal your impulses
Behind the unintentional echoes of your dejection.
As sticks and stones may break my bones,
So too do your words wound me.
You proclaim yourself unpredictable,
But all I see is negligence and reluctance.
The contradictions in our nature—
My endeavor and pride, your apathy and hesitation;
My tenderness and restraint, your firmness and

indulgence—
Make us perfect complements.
Bound to coalesce into one another,
Yielding a spectrum of hues and colors,
To fill our drowning lives
And metamorphose them
Into an ecstatic, intriguing odyssey.

13. In An Alternate Universe

Maybe in an alternate universe,
somewhere in a distant galaxy,
there exists a world—
of light, laughter, hope, and endless possibility,
where you are mine, forever, till eternity.
Maybe in that world,
my eyes won't be dull, sunken, or tired,
no longer chasing your fading shadows—
but shining instead,
reflecting the radiance of your face.
There, I would hold your hand,
walk with you through city streets,
from "The Raoucheh" to "Downtown",
instead of wandering alone in my mind,
keeping our old conversations alive like sacred echoes.
My restless soul
running through wilderness,
camping on high mountains,
traversing jungles,
drowning in the depths of the ocean,
sailing through the unknown,
would finally find its peaceful rest,
in your arms.

14. Let the Moon Sink

Let the moon sink
into the dullness of my eyes,
let the sun never rise again,
Just like that day
when you didn't show up.
Let time stop,
let Earth's revolution and rotation cease,
trapping me in this moment.
This moment of vulnerability,
this moment of truth.
I'm tired of pretending
it doesn't hurt anymore.
But it does.
And it always will.
Will the pain fade
only when the universe itself ceases to exist?

15. When Was The Last Time

When was the last time
you held my hand, walking close,
slowing your steps
just so we could stay together
a few seconds longer?
When was the last time
you called my name and stopped me,
just as I was about to disappear,
only to steal one more look at my face?
When was the last time
you stared at me with those gloomy eyes,
love, fondness, and passion
rolling down your cheeks as tears?
When was the last time
you thought of me..?
saw vivid pictures of us
etched in memory, clear even with closed eyes?
When was the last time
you felt that you were mine,
and I was yours..!!
beyond the conventional definitions of love,
beyond the boundaries of distance, time, and space?

16. Oh Girl, Dare To Dream

Oh girl, dare to dream—
all over again.
For it only ends when you die.
Unfold your wings, unleash your thoughts,
and fly high—
all over again.
For it only ends when you die.
Do not let society, nor its people,
subdue you—for a girl you are.
This is what you must change,
this struggle is your destiny.
They may bury you beneath responsibilities,
for you are a daughter and a wife.
But that is not all you were meant to be.
Of all, you have the honor,
the distinction to bear a child,
to be a mother—
and for that child, the safest place
is not in its father's arms, but in yours—
your touch, your presence.
For it knows—
you are not a victim of society,
but its mother.
Bravest of them all, strongest of them all.

To mistake your tenderness,
your kindness, your forgiveness for weakness
is the shallowest folly of all.
For what it's worth, I do not know.
But listen to me, oh girl, one last time:
It's never too late.
It only ends when we die.
So, dare—dare to fly high.
Chase the sunlight, love the moonlight.
Travel the cosmos, infinite.
For you are a girl—
a girl who dares to dream.

17. RISE AND SHINE

Oh, my lady, rise and shine,
for now is the time.
Oh, my lady,
this society and its people are onto you.
Listen—there are sounds of struggle
traveling through the air,
and a river red is flowing everywhere.
The floor beneath you burns, hot as fire.
Come to me, stay by my side—
you too must burn
in the hell they've ignited into my flesh.
Because I fight from your side.
Oh, my lady, rise and shine,
for now is the time
to show the world that your eyes aren't only for tears,
but for beautiful, spectacular dreams.
That your hands aren't only for donning engagement
rings,
but to strive and fulfil your desires.
You are not just to be described
with adjectives of beauty and charm,
but with strength, courage, and valour too.
You must change the perception of how they define you.
Oh, my lady, rise and shine,

for now is the time.

Break the handcuffs,

free yourself from the shackles of femininity

that society tries to tame you with.

Oh, my lady, rise and shine,

for now is the time.

Time does not wait, and I too am a mortal who will die.

So before this moment passes by,

hold my hand and run.

The whole world awaits us—

 let's go and chase our happiness, **Infinity across Infinity**

18. The Girl with Giggles And A Dragon Tattoo

The Girl with Giggles
And rebellious thoughts,
Dreams unconventional,
An enthusiasm to break free
From all the world's insane boundaries.
The girl with a heart—pure and undead,
Manners sometimes sly,
Wanting to capture moments of joy,
Daring to take leaps of faith,
Willing to go beyond prescribed confines.
The girl with a dragon tattoo on her arm—
And if not a beauty mark,
Then a medal of honor,
Carved into flesh—some called it a scar,
Yet it spoke of how she not only survived, but thrived.
She was no plastic blonde doll,
Waiting for a prince charming,
Kissing frogs in fairytales.
She was a pirate—one who gave no damn
For any omen about *"a woman on a ship."*
An invader of unconquered oceans,
A seeker of never-seen lands.
The girl I once met.

The girl she once was.

The girl I shall always remember her as.

19. I See You

We may be far away in distance and time,
but I see you—
in the soothing light of the moon,
and the morning sky's bright blue.
I see you—
in the cute smiles of toddlers,
and in the warmth of blessings from the elderly.
And at work, when everything goes south,
I see you at the North Wall—
with your head held high, standing tall,
telling me in an inspiring tone:
"Don't stop when you're tired, stop when you're done."
I see you—
with eyes closed, at a hand's distance.
I wish to hold your hand, but I don't—
because it's the distance that tells me
how close I want us to be,
how important you are,
how it does not matter where I am, or where you are.
You're always in my mind and in my heart.
I see you—
in everywhere I go,
and in everything I do.

20. The Night's Dilemma

Everything is still.
Not a whisper of breeze can be felt.
An old, settled monster
has come back into my dreams.
As the Joker says,
"This is what happens,
when an unstoppable force meets an immovable object."
A vicious circle
of never-ending pain.
I keep moving away,
but shadows keep chasing.
They toss and turn,
I hide and run.
Time passes
but nothing changes.
Is this a night
that will never see a sunrise?

21. A Love Beyond Time

Months and years pass,
Moments and memories fade,
Situations change, time moves on.
Dreams, fears, inspirations come and go.
Almost everything is transient—
Even our lives in this world.
But, my **Mry** (An Egyptian for 'beloved'),
I will let you in on a secret.
There is one thing I know
To be permanent, eternal—
My unconditional love for you.
If not this year, then maybe the next.
If not in this life, then perhaps in the next.
You and I will be us—together, forever.
And I cannot help but wonder
How that life would be.
Now tell me, oh my lady,
Do you want to see what I see?
A starry night sky, a crescent moon,
Magical stardust sprinkling over us.
Hand in hand, we walk through a garden
Where memories of our past bloom like flowers—
A thousand conversations, a thousand colors,
A thousand promises, a thousand scents.

We reach a mystical blue lake,

Where folklores whisper of fairies

Who dance and play music at night.

We sit on a rock, fingers entwined,

Your head resting gently on my shoulder.

Forgetting the world, its people, its noise—

Lost in each other, as we were meant to be.

And in that moment,

A tear rolls down my cheek,

Then onto yours,

Before finally resting on your lips.

Time stops.

But do you know the real beauty of it?

This is not the end.

This is how the story goes on and on.

This is how destiny is fulfilled.

It may seem like an impossible dream,

But so be it.

For what good is reality, If it means living without you?